His moms

FREELOADERS

By:Anthony Hawkins

ISBN:978-1-312-29883-5

Cover Art By Anthony Hawkins

Dedicated to the gay and lesbian community.

Prologue

Javion was 21 years old and lived alone with his mother Pam who mostly worked night shifts while he worked day shifts parttime,and also attending afternoon classes on most weekdays.

Chapter 1

It was a friday afternoon and Javion was working on one of his homework assignments dealing with world history as Pam entered the house through the front door with grocery bags in her hands.

I got you ma,Javion quickly rose from the sofa and his homework assignment to help Pam with the grocery bags,Javion placing the grocery bags on the kitchen counter as Pam kicked her shoes off her feet into a corner of the living area,taking a huge sigh of relief.How your day was,you alright? Javion questioned Pam as he placed the groceries away.It was alright,im just a little tired,and this lady at the store got on my nerves today,i swear she did,Pam spoke to Javion,stress on her face.Ay baby go hold the door open for Alonzo and Malik,they helping me with some bags,it's more bags in the car,Pam spoke to Javion.

Why you just aint ask me to help you? Javion spoke to Pam with a sort of annoyed facial expression.I knew you would probably be in here doing school work so i didn't want to bother you,Malik and Alonzo got it,just finish your homework,they good help,even tho i know they just doing it because they want a few dollars in their pockets,they good boys tho,Pam explained to Javion.I wish you would've asked me to help you,i cant stand them dudes,they stay talking trash,Javion spoke to Pam with annoyance,Pam chuckling a bit afterwards.Them boys aint got much family so try and be nice to them ok,and i told them they could spend the night,its just for the night,Alonzo aunt kicked him out,he 19,he aint that much younger than you,and Malik just turned 19 too,at least you got some boys close to your age to hangout with,Pam spoke to Javion.

I already got friends ma,dont need new ones,you know i dont like them dudes,but im going try and tolerate them for tonight,Javion spoke to Pam,disgust on his face,Javion not being too fond of the two young men Malik and Alonzo.Malik and Alonzo were two young men who occasionally helped Javion's mother with groceries and other things,and tho they were both rough around the edges Pam still saw some potential in them both,tho with Javion it was a different story in itself.

Javion headed to the front door to hold it open just as Pam told him,his eyes watching the two young men Alonzo and Malik approaching the house from the car with grocery bags swinging from their fingers.Ms pam where you want us to put these? One of the young men spoke.Just put it right there over on the counter,thanks baby,you a real help Malik,Pam spoke to the young man very politely.Alonzo close that door for me baby,Pam then spoke to the other young man,the young man obeying.

Well,im about to go take my ass a nap before i go to work later on,yall two make yall selves at home,food in the fridge,cable tv,just ask Javion if yall need anything,and thank yall again,Pam handed both Malik and Alonzo twenty dollar bills,a warm nurturing facial expression on her face.Thanks maam,both Malik and Alonzo spoke politely to Pam,Pam smiling and then heading into her bedroom.

Look at this faggot ass nigga,Malik spoke to Alonzo after Pam fled the living area,Malik's homophobic slur referring to Javion,Alonzo then snickering at the derogatory slur.Really dude,you broke as fuck,and you dirty as shit,all you and Alonzo do is freeload off my mother,dirty ass niggas,Javion spoke harshly to Malik,a frown on his face.Nigga shut your gay ass up,we know you suck dick,just like your moms suck my dick the other night,i bet she would give me that head if i wanted it,Alonzo spoke to Javion with a smug smirk.Leave my moms outta this,i should tell her what you said,and you know damn well she wouldn't touch your dirty ass with a ten foot pole,you deluding yourself dude,thats why your aunt kicked your stupid ass out,Javion spoke to Alonzo.

Nigga mind your business,little dick sucking ass nigga,Alonzo spoke angrily to Javion,Javion's words sort of getting to him.Fuck that dick in the booty ass nigga Lonzo,let's go get up in the fridge dawg,Malik spoke to Alonzo.Nigga you lucky we up in your mama house or i would've kicked your ass man,Alonzo spoke to Javion,and then heading off to the kitchen with Malik.Javion headed back over to the sofa to finish with

his homework as Alonzo and Malik
raided the fridge.

Chapter 2

The hours passed,and soon it was
time for Pam to head off to work,tho
she wished she didn't have to.Alright
boys,im going trust yall to be good
while im gone tonight,no girls over
either,Pam spoke to
Malik,Alonzo,and Javion with a
smile.We got you,we all grown,you
just have a good night at work,and
thanks again for letting us spend the

night ms Pam,Malik spoke to
Pam,Malik putting on a charming act
in front of Pam.

Try to be nice,Pam whispered to
Javion as she kissed him on the
cheek,and then heading out the front
door to work,leaving all of the young
men home alone.

Pam had no idea that Malik and
Alonzo weren't as innocent and
charming as she thought,tho Javion
indeed knew this himself,Javion
seeing Malik and Alonzo as

hoodlums,while Pam saw them as bad little boys in need of guidance.

You a mamas boy ass nigga dawg,you still getting kisses and shit from your moms and shit,bitch made ass nigga,Malik spoke to Javion with a light smirk.Nigga why you mad tho,because you aint got no mom? Javion spoke to Malik with sarcasm.Nigga just deal with the fact that you a faggy ass nigga man,thats what you do dawg,Malik spoke to Javion,Alonzo chuckling afterwards.Anyway,im about to go take a shower,fuck yall to stink ass motherfuckers,im out,Javion spoke to both Malik and Alonzo,and then heading off into the bathroom to shower.Yea nigga,you need to shower,so you can rinse all that nut off your mouth,Alonzo insulted Javion as Javion headed into the bathroom,Javion ignoring him.

Javion was a homosexual male,tho a lot of people would assume he was a heterosexual male,only a few of Javion's friends knew of his sexual orientation,and Malik and Alonzo knew of it as well,tho they weren't his friends,Pam herself was oblivious of Javion's sexual orientation.Javion was a very handsome young man,having white teeth,full lips,a tall toned body,very smooth baby soft chocolate brown colored skin,and soft dark thick and shiny hair that was cut short and neat.

Malik and Alonzo weren't bad looking young men themselves,Malik being dark chocolate brown skin with very full dark and seductive and plump lips,a youthful mature and handsome but rough and intimidating face,and a strong and lean and tall toned body,his hair cut short and covered with a black durag,thin and soft facial hair curving over his top lip,and Alonzo was an attractive young man as well,having chocolate brown skin,a short and neat box shaped haircut,a handsome and strong smooth shaven square shaped face,and a tall muscular but not overdone body,and an earring in both his ears,and a tiny tattoo on his upper arm.

Javion began to take off all of his clothes after he entered the bathroom,his hand twisting on the showerhead as he stepped his completely naked body into the bathtub.The hot water exiting from the showerhead rained down on Javion's nude body as he soaped himself up thoroughly,his eyes closed shut as he placed his face directly under the hot raining showerhead.

Javion's eyes opened as he heard someone enter the bathroom,his face moving away from the showerhead.Somebody in here? Javion questioned whoever it was that had entered the bathroom.Nigga stop trippin,your scared punk ass,im just taking a leak nigga,Alonzo spoke to Javion,Javion then hearing trickling sounds pouring into the toilet as he continued to shower himself.A short second later Alonzo quickly pulled the shower curtain back with his exposed penis in his hand as Javion stood shocked and naked inside the bathtub,the showerhead still pouring down on Javion's wet and soapy exposed body.

Here go your shower nigga! Alonzo began to urinate on Javion as Javion shouted out in shock and disgust.You is a nasty motherfucker,i swear man! Javion yelled at Alonzo with anger,disgust all over his face,and a mischievous grin on Alonzo's face.Javion turned the showerhead towards Alonzo,letting the showerhead sprinkle onto Alonzo's clothes as Alonzo shouted out loudly in shock,the showerhead drenching Alonzo and his clothes with water.Stop playing man! Alonzo yelled out,not wanting him or his clothes to get wet any longer.Good nigga,thats what your ass get,Javion chuckled out sinisterly to Alonzo,Javion feeling he had gotten even with Alonzo for Alonzo's foul and tasteless urinating prank.

Here you go nigga! Javion turned the water temperature on cold as Alonzo shouted out in deep shock from the cold water streaming onto him from the showerhead,vengeful satisfaction on Javion's face.Stop nigga,what the fuck?! Alonzo shouted to Javion as he quickly ran out of the bathroom from Javion and the raining showerhead soaking wet,his clothes sticking to his body.

Chapter 3

Javion cackled out loud after his own watery prank on Alonzo,and then turning the water temperature back to hot as he continued with his hot shower,Alonzo swearing in the other room as Malik laughed at him.Javion washed and soaped himself thoroughly as he let the suds cleanse every nook and cranny of his exposed body,and then rinsing himself off.Javion stepped gently out of the bathtub after he was done with his long and hot steamy shower,water slowly trickling down his nude wet body as he reached for a towel to dry himself off.

Javion placed the short white towel tightly around the waist of his toned naked body and then slipped his damp feet into shower shoes as he exited the bathroom into the living area.Javion headed into the kitchen for a slim bottle of water as he passed Malik by on the sofa watching the television set and then passing Alonzo by as Alonzo shook the water from his clothes.

Nigga you wrong dawg,look what you did to my clothes tho,Alonzo spoke to

Javion as he continued to shake the water from his wet clothes.Nigga you would've wet my clothes up and i would've whooped your ass cuz,Malik spoke to Javion as he turned his attention to him,Malik then tensing up a bit as he examined Javion's sculpted naked body in nothing but a short above knee white towel and shower shoes.Malik took his eyes off of Javion for a second and then stared at him once more,a tense and strange expression on his face.Your gay ass,Malik spoke to Javion,but not with as much volume and depth as he usually did.

Yea,i like dudes,i love them actually,i like to do this to them too,Javion spoke to Malik as he twirled the slim water bottle tip in his mouth seductively and provocatively with his eyes directly on Malik,Javion hoping to make Malik feel uncomfortable and disgusted with his display of pretend homosexual acts as he thought a homophobic heterosexual male would be about it,Javion pretending that the bottle was that of a male sex organ.

You gay man,eww dawg,Malik spoke to Javion with deep tension surging throughout his fidgeting body.Damn this joint taste good dawg,Javion continued to tease Malik as he slowly licked and pretended to practically make out with the water bottle with his mouth and tongue,Malik pulling a decorative pillow from the sofa onto his lap as he watched him.Faggot ass nigga man,Malik spoke to Javion as he slightly twitched and fidgeted tensely on the sofa,his face revealing uncomfort and unease,Javion snickering at his discomfort.Dawg go get me a towel or something man,so i can get my clothes dry and shit man,help me out dawg,Alonzo spoke to Malik,Malik not budging.Dawg help me cuz,Alonzo spoke to Malik again,Malik refusing to get up as he ignored Alonzo.

Dawg im watching the tv cuz,stop bugging man! Malik spoke to Alonzo with annoyance and discomfort.You acting funny cuz,Alonzo spoke to Malik,and then catching Javion acting provocatively with the water bottle out of the corner of his eye,his face nearly dropping in shock.Dawg you is gay as fuck son,and put some clothes on my dude,you disrespectful dawg,Alonzo chuckled lightly to Javion as he examined him.

Im about to leave yall two niggas out here,im about to go hit the shower,both yall dudes on some other shit man,Malik spoke to Alonzo and Javion as he rose from the sofa and then into the bathroom.Eww,nigga put your clothes back on,Javion spoke to Alonzo as he saw him beginning to undress from his wet clothes.You wet my shit up dawg,im going hop in the shower after Malik get done,if you going be naked i can too,Alonzo spoke to Javion as he peeled himself out of his clothes,his hard naked body flashing before Javion's eyes.Javion felt a bit uncomfortable standing there practically naked along with Alonzo,Javion not used to seeing another naked male this close to him and the male not being gay.

What you see something you like? Alonzo spoke to javion as he smirked.Dawg you aint hardly got anything i want,Javion spoke to Alonzo.Whatever man,Alonzo spoke to Javion as he walked passed him,Alonzo grazing Javion's shoulder on purpose as he walked by.

Malik exited the bathroom after his shower in nothing but an above knee white towel and a pair of shower shoes on his feet,his abs flexing,his tall lean and strong body damp,and his legs strong,his body smelling of fresh soap as did Javion's.Alonzo headed into the bathroom to shower himself as Javion and Malik occupied the living area.Yall got any deodorant around this joint? Malik moved closer to Javion,their exposed bodies nearly making contact.Go check in the closet

in the hallway,Javion spoke to
Malik.Your bitch ass,come on,let's
fight dawg,yall gay niggas cant throw
a punch,Malik began to playfully
strike Javion in his exposed abs,Javion
buckling back a bit with a lack of
interest.Malik pushed his shoulder
onto Javion's as his cheek grazed
along Javion's gently in a caress,Malik
playfully and smoothly and mildly
tussling with Javion as they both
became very silent,Malik biting down
on his bottom lip in the process.

Im not into that faggot shit,but you
ever let a dude bust in your mouth?

Malik whispered to Javion.Naw,that aint none of your business,you and Alonzo stay talking shit,but now you trying be all buddy buddy with me now,Javion spoke to Malik.Dawg stop being sensitive,sometimes i be fucking around with you,thats why i cant stand some of yall gay niggas,Malik spoke to Javion.I bet your hands not even bigger than mine,Malik snatched up Javion's hand and then comparing them in size,Malik seeing that his hand was actually just a bit bigger than Javion's.And im taller than you,Malik boasted about himself being a bit taller than Javion as well,Malik seeming as if he was trying to find any reason he could possible to touch Javion.

Yall fags out here,Alonzo joked as he exited the bathroom with nothing but a short white towel around his naked waist and thick flip flops on his big feet.Them niggas be tapping your ass nigga,thats why your ass so phat dawg,not that im looking at it,im just saying,your ass fatter than most girls i know cuz,my moms told me that mean a dude gay,Alonzo spoke to Javion as he studied Javion's firm and tight and round above knee length towel covered buttocks area,his tongue licking his lips slightly.

I was with this one chick and she was trying give me and my homeboy main man Malik the pussy and head,you be doing shit like that with other niggas dawg,you be letting niggas hit you from two ways? Alonzo spoke to Javion with curiosity.I remember that dawg,them gay niggas probably cant give head better than no female i bet,them gay niggas be faking cuz,i bet that shit aint even true,Malik spoke to Alonzo slyly,Alonzo agreeing.We should rough this nigga up for talking all that shit he be talking Lonzo,Malik spoke to Alonzo.Fuck yea we should,Alonzo agreed with Malik.

Malik gently bumped his body onto the front of Javion's body as Alonzo bumped his body onto the back of Javion's body,all of their exposed chests and short white towels and exposed thighs meeting in a bumpy trio friction.Stop playing yall,Javion spoke to both Malik and Alonzo,Javion feeling they were acting like juveniles.Get off me dawg,Javion gently bumped his towel covered buttocks onto Alonzo's towel covered crotch area,Javion thinking that would stop Alonzo from being up close behind him,Javion thinking Alonzo would be offended by it,tho Alonzo pushed his crotch onto Javion's buttocks further and heavier,his head curving closely around Javion's neck as his breathing got heavier.

Nigga we aint going do nothing to you dawg,stop acting like a pussy man,we was just playing with you son,we know you like dudes dawg,we aint about to jump you or nothing man,we respect your fucking moms,but stop faking dawg,let me and my dude fuck,Alonzo moaned very silently in Javion's ear as Javion felt him press up even tighter behind him.You pissed on me man,and you think im going get down with yall dude? Javion spoke to Alonzo.Dawg you was already in the shower,and you clean now,we all clean dawg,i can go first and then Malik can go next,im going just nut quick,Alonzo moaned in Javion's ear.

Malik and Alonzo both began to kiss all over Javion as he began to flutter on the inside,tho Javion wasn't always on good terms with Malik and Alonzo he was still somewhat sexually attracted to them both at the moment,Javion seeing and feeling a somewhat softer and warmer side of Malik and Alonzo,a side of them he had never seen before.Malik and Alonzo were the discreet sexually adventurous type,the type that suppressed and harbored their attraction for the same sex out of fear,that playing a role in to why they both sometimes picked on Javion.

Just get on the couch dude,and i go first,Alonzo guided Javion and himself onto the sofa,his hands firmly around Javion's waist.Naw dude,i can handle both of yall dudes,Javion spoke to Alonzo,Javion becoming just as aroused as Alonzo and Malik were.Oh word dawg,thats whats up,you can handle both them dicks then dude,right here on your mama couch bruh,Alonzo moaned to Javion in arousal.Malik sat down on the sofa as he unwrapped the towel from around the waist of his naked body,his body strong built and tall,and his penis swinging nearly as big as his lean body.You aint about that life cuz,let me see if you can really suck on a dick like you was doing that bottle dawg,Malik moaned deeply to Javion as Javion gently grabbed ahold of Malik's hardened penis.

Malik bit down on his lip in lust and pleasure as Javion smoothly and firmly placed his penis into his wet and warm mouth.Get that nigga ass while i get that mouth Alonzo,Malik spoke to Alonzo.Alonzo pulled the towel from around the waist of Javion's naked body and then pulled off his own from his naked body as he let both their towels fall to the sofa.Alonzo licked his hand and then stroked and massaged his slinky huge penis with it,and then smoothly entering his strong and huge penis inbetween Javion's inner warm and fleshy walls,his mouth widening in pleasure as he felt himself fit deeply inside of Javion,his strong hand forcing Javion's back to arch a bit as he laid down on him.Javion took Malik's hard penis into his mouth in huge gulps as Alonzo deeply drilled into him from behind,all three of their naked smooth brown bodies intertwined in a heated group orgy.

Suck that shit dawg! Malik shoved Javion's head smoothly up and down on his penis,gagging sounds and sounds of naked flesh slapping against naked flesh and loud moans of sexual thrill filling the room as Javion,Malik,and Alonzo all went at it hard and heavy.Alonzo turned Javion over on his back easily,and then pushed himself back into Javion with strong strokes of his hard stabbing penis as Malik began to fastly thrust his penis back and forth into Javion's mouth from the side,Javion's mouth and Malik's penis meeting in choking sounds.Javion felt sort of guilty and naughty about what he and Malik and Alonzo were doing,but it extremely turned him on.

Open up that nigga ass dawg! Malik coached Alonzo on as he enjoyed himself as well.Suck that dick like i had a gun to your head nigga! Malik moaned out deeply to Javion as Javion continued to take his penis into his mouth whole,Javion receiving a hard mouthful of Malik as Alonzo plunged into him back and forth in an intense friction and rocking rhythm,Alonzo's tight strong and lean nude body moving up and down on top of Javion's toned nude body.Javion felt that Malik and Alonzo were a bit more aggressive and hardcore than his usual male lovers,but it didn't bother him.

Alonzo pulled Javion's leg further up as he dug deeper into him,Malik muffling Javion's moans of internal pleasure with his thick penis,Javion's throat constricting back and forth to the size of it.Javion could feel his loins heating up and throbbing in ecstasy and pleasure as he was probed by both young men at the same time,the nerve points inside of Javion being massaged and plucked the right way.The heat fuming from Javion,Malik,and Alonzo's naked bodies warmed the sofa.

You a slut ass nigga dawg,thats whats up! Malik moaned out to Javion as he trembled close to an eruption inside of Javion's mouth.Nigga you probably aint never had real hood niggas dick before,you used to them sissy niggas cuz,take that motherfucking dick dawg,earn respect for you gay niggas cuz,Alonzo traveled throughout Javion's body with the insanely intense pleasure of Javion's tight inner walls tightly hugging his penis,Javion's feet slightly touching Alonzo's hard flexing buttocks.

Let me rape that mouth nigga! the words deeply dragged from Malik's lips to Javion,Malik deeply dipping and popping his throbbing penis a few more times deep into Javion's mouth until he intensely ejaculated into Javion's mouth in loud moans of pleasure,Javion squeezing his lips together tightly around Malik's pulsating penis as Malik's semen erupted into his mouth,nearly filling it up.Let me see that nut in your mouth,Malik ordered Javion to open his mouth in a deep exhale,Malik liking the look of Javion's used and abused mouth.Javion opened his mouth to Malik and then let Malik watch as he swallowed his warm substances,Javion then giving Malik's still shooting and sensually stimulated and now sensitive penis one more lick and gulp across the shaft and tip as Malik gasped out in a shock of pleasure.

Javion could feel Alonzo's hot substances heavily shoot and flow into him as he swallowed the last bit of Malik's,Alonzo quietly clenching his lips together as he ejaculated into Javion in silent pleasure,both he and Javion staring intimately eye to eye,the hot naked flesh of their bodies still connected as Javion erupted with an exciting orgasm of his own.

Thanks dawg,Malik gave Javion a strong highfive as he deeply inhaled and exhaled to the sofa cushions,Malik showing gratitude for their sexual encounter.Alonzo wiped himself and Javion down with one of the towels and then laid to the sofa,Javion still laying on his back as he stared up at the ceiling in silent breaths.You a cool dude dawg,Alonzo complimented Javion silently as they all laid on the sofa.Oh so now im a cool dude? Javion snickered a bit,the room then filling with the silent snickers of Javion,Malik,and Alonzo as they all laid to the sofa in their full nudity and satisfaction.

Chapter 4

Ay cuz we should do this on a regular basis,Malik spoke to both Javion and Alonzo as they all laid naked to the sofa.Im with that man,Alonzo agreed with Malik.Yea,that sound cool,Javion then agreed with Malik and Alonzo.What time your moms get off work bruh? Malik questioned Javion.She usually get home around like 11:00 or 10:00 in the morning,Javion spoke to Malik.I got you cuz,so we should be cool for awhile,because its only like 10:45 now,we good until the morning,im trying fuck again,this time i want the ass homey,my dude got it last time,Malik spoke to Javion.

Yall trying turn a nigga into a hoe and shit,Javion joked with Malik,Malik chuckling a bit afterwards.Malik and Alonzo both were very vibrant and energetic and very sexually vigorous young men who craved sexual pleasure just as much as any other typical young man did,even more than Javion himself.

Let me hit the back this time cuz,on no bullshit,Malik spoke to Javion,his face serious.Let's get it popping cuz,i wanna see what that mouth working with,Alonzo spoke to Javion.Alright,Javion spoke innocently to Alonzo and Malik,Agreeing to have another sexual encounter with them both before Pam got home in the morning.Javion and Malik and Alonzo's naked bodies all moved close to each other as their sexual arousal began to ascend once more,Javion,Malik,and Alonzo all touching each other provocatively.

Javion,Malik,and Alonzo all suddenly jumped in fear as they heard keys enter into the front door of the house,their bodies quickly departing from each other as Pam entered the front door with a face full of shock,tho Javion and the others moved quickly,they didn't move quickly enough for Pam to not see that there was something sexual in nature that was indeed about to happen before she unexpectedly entered.

Oh,hey ms Pam,we was all chilling! Malik stuttered nervously to Pam out of fear of being caught.Hey ma,i thought you was at work,what you doing home so early? Javion spoke nervously and guiltily to Pam as he and Malik and Alonzo all backed into a corner of the sofa naked and holding onto their exposed sex organs with their hands to cover themselves.Pam knew she had unknowingly interrupted something mutually sexual between Javion,Malik and Alonzo but she had a hard time wrapping her mind around it,she was in utter shock of it all.Hey ms Pam,you alright,how was work? Alonzo spoke nervously and stutteringly to Pam in hopes to ease her shock and change the subject of the matter between them all.

Dont nobody talk right now,please,my head hurting now,Pam spoke to Alonzo and the others as she slightly held onto her forehead in aw.Yall then gave me a real surprise tonight i tell you,im still trying get myself together,i clocked outta work early today and then come home to this,phew,Pam spoke to all three young men.Yall need to leave the living room for a minute while i get my head right,im talking to yall two,i catch yall and my son all naked together like yall about to do the nasty and get yall freak on,and then yall little dingalings got a nerve to be hardened up,aint no need in hiding them now,little nasty behinds,yall go in the other room while i have a talk with Javion,me and this one going have a long talk,Pam spoke to Alonzo and Malik sternly,Pam having mixed emotions on her catching Javion,Alonzo,and Malik in a provocative situation,a small part of Pam disturbed,but most of all shocked.

We sorry ms Pam,both Alonzo and Malik spoke to Pam as they got up from Javion and the sofa to leave the area on Pam's command,their faces guilty and mournful,and their hands still covering their male sex organs as their nude bodies headed into the other room,Javion still sitting silently and nervously on the sofa in his nudity as he awaited Pam's assumed scolding.Aint no need in hiding your stuff,i already seen it before,i just wanna know what was going on up in here,tell me something? Pam spoke to Javion more calmer than he expected.Me and Alonzo and Malik was about to call some girls over,you know what else,Javion lied to Pam,Pam already knowing that he was lying to her,her motherly intuition telling her another story,and what she saw with her own eyes telling her another story as well.

Boy dont sit there and lie to me,i saw yall,all of yall,aint no girls in sight,and all yall butt ass naked,i aint no fool baby,i was once your age,just tell me the truth,i aint going get mad,Pam slightly smirked at Javion.You gay,you attracted to other boys,do you get a feeling in your wee wee for them?

Pam questioned Javion seriously.Javion hesitated to answer Pam's question,but then finally said something.Yea,im gay ma,i been like this ever since i was little man,i knew i was different,Javion admitted his same sex attraction silently and shamefully to Pam as she listened to him carefully with all ears.Aint nothing to be ashamed of,you should remember when i told you God love everybody,old,young,sick,black,white ,it dont matter to him baby,we all people of God,Jesus love everybody,and i'll always love you unconditionally,thats what a mother does,come here,Pam took Javion into her arms in a huge embrace,Javion smiling inside,Javion feeling that a load had been lifted off of him.

I was just watching that it gets better project thing on tv awhile back,and it really hit a nerve in me,Pam spoke to Javion.And another thing,dont think im done with you,you better had used a condom if yall did do something,your first time if this is should at least be special,and not cheap,now that im done with you,im going get their black asses too,just like i got your black ass,Pam spoke to

Javion with a thin smile,Javion smiling back.

Javion wrapped his short white towel back around the waist of his naked body as he slid his feet back into his shower shoes and then headed into his bedroom with his spirits high,Pam playfully slapping him on his backside as he fled.

Pam then called for Alonzo and Malik as she sat down in a dining room chair.Man she about to kick us out cuz,Malik spoke to Alonzo in fear and silence.Naw dawg,she cool,but i hope she dont,alonzo spoke back to Malik.Nigga you stupid as fuck,we gangbanged her son,you really think she going let us stay here after that dawg,get real cuz,Malik spoke to Alonzo with annoyance.Malik and Alonzo's silent conversation stopped as they entered the room with Pam silently and nervously.Here,cover yall junk up,Pam tossed Malik and Alonzo towels as they stood before her nude and afraid and nervous.Malik and Alonzo quickly placed the short white towels around their naked waists as they waited for Pam to swear at them or at least kick them out.

Im disappointed at yall,im not going lie,i thought yall would probably be like brothers to Javion,but that then flew out the window now,but yall still young,and like i told Javion i was once yall age,so dont trip,all yall grown so i cant really tell yall so much,im not going cuss yall out,Javion still my baby,no matter how old he is,so to see yall laid up with him kind of made my head spin,i aint mad tho,just try and be more private about yall little business,at least until i clear my head,i dont wanna have to cut one of yall little wee wees off now,Pam spoke playfully to Malik and Alonzo as they listened to her with obedience.Im done with yall,yall go get dressed or something,do whatever,my damn head hurt,i need a cigarette,Pam spoke to Malik and Alonzo.Thank you ms Pam,and like for real tho im sorry,and i didn't force nothing on javion,he cool people maam,Malik spoke to Pam.Im sorry too ms Pam,Alonzo then spoke to Pam,his face apologetic.

Im still shocked that all yall gay or experimenting,when i was growing up my gay friends used to be out there,they could switch,do hair,dress better,and wear more lip gloss than me,but yall still boy boys if that make any sense,the world is full of surprises,im about to take my ass to sleep,i guess i see yall later,yall still welcome to stay,all of yall played a role in what happened tonight,Pam spoke to Malik and Alonzo as she got up and then headed into her bedroom,leaving Malik and Alonzo alone in the living area.

Malik and Alonzo were relieved that Pam didn't take their provocative situation with Javion as bad as they thought she would,neither one of them wanting to leave the house.Everyone eventually slept silently that night,and no grudges were held.

Chapter 5

The weeks passed and Javion had begun to develope a brotherhood and deep purely sexual relationship with both Malik and Alonzo,they were even more careful not to get caught.It was a late saturday night and Javion and Malik,and Alonzo were all playing around naked in the shower while Pam was at work,Alonzo spraying Javion and Malik down with the cold raining showerhead as they yelled and ducked in shock and laughter.Javion got more in touch with his fun and playful side as he hung out with Malik and Alonzo more and more.

Yall faggy ass niggas! Alonzo chased Javion and Malik out into the living area as he whipped them with a towel,their naked bodies glistening with tiny drops of water.Dawg we getting the floor wet! Javion cautioned Alonzo.Nigga shut your punk ass up! Alonzo whipped Javion's exposed buttocks with the towel swinging from his hand,Javion shouting in a slight sting of pain and humor,Alonzo and Malik snickering humorously in response.Javion flinched as he heard someone begin to knock loudly on the front door of the house,Alonzo and Malik turning their attention to the door as well.Quit man,hold up,let me get the door right quick,Javion spoke to

Alonzo.Javion quickly pulled a short above knee length white towel around the waist of his naked sculpted body as he shoved his damp feet into shower shoes to answer the front door,Alonzo and malik still playing around naked in the background.

Who is it? Javion answered the front door as he peeped out the peephole.It's Quinton from down the street,is ms Pam in? The knocker spoke in a male voice outside of the front door.Naw,she out right now,can i take a message? Javion spoke to the male outside the door.Yea,ms Pam told me to stop pass here,i was supposed to come fix the drain in her bathroom,the man spoke to Javion.Hold on for a second dude,my bad,Javion spoke to the man as he reached for his cellphone next to the dining room table as it charged.

Javion pressed speed dial on his cellphone and then waited patiently for the person he called to answer his call as it rang.Hello? Pam's voice answered javion's call.Hey,this dude outside the door said you asked him to come and fix the shower drain in your room,im just checking with you before i open the door for this dude,you know him? Javion spoke to Pam.Yea,thats Quinton,yall used to play together when yall was little,you probably dont remember him tho,but go ahead and let him in,bye,i gotta get back to work,Pam spoke to Javion and then ending their call.Javion placed his cellphone back onto the dining room table and then slowly opened the front door to let the young man Quinton in.

Quinton's face became slightly flushed and tense as Javion stood naked and wet right before him at the doorway in nothing but a short white towel and a pair of shower shoes on his feet as he swung open the door to let him inside.Ay dude,whats good,can you point me to yall bathroom? the young man Quinton spoke to Javion in a slight tense stutter,Javion's nakedness kind of distracting him and putting him in an uncomfortable position.

Quinton was a handsome clean and soft brown skin young man with long neatly locked and well kept dreadlocks that swung down on each side of his very smooth hairless and strong oval shaped face,his smile warm and attractive,and his tall and slightly slender and strong body dressed in a black overshirt and a pair of denim jeans,nike shoes on his feet,and a small toolbox swinging from his hand.

Quinton tried hard not to focus on javion's exposed body but he didn't want to be rude and stare away while he was talking to Javion,Quinton's eyes seeing Javion's smooth chocolate brown colored exposed supple pecks and smooth and toned abs,and then Javion's long toned and strong smooth legs that protruded from the short above knee length white towel around the firm waist of his naked body.My bad for bothering you homey,i didn't know you was in the shower,Quinton spoke to Javion.Oh naw,it's cool man,just come in,the bathroom down there to the left,Javion spoke to Quinton politely,pointing Quinton to Pam's bathroom.Thanks homey,Quinton spoke to Javion and then spotting Alonzo and Malik playfully whipping each other with towels in their nakedness as he tensed up even more.

Quinton headed back to Pam's bedroom as he kept his head turned,Quinton pretending as if he didn't see Javion,Malik,and Alonzo casually walking around in only nothing but towels and their nudity,his face and entire body tense.Ay yall put some towels on,i think we making that dude feel uncomfortable,he probably calling us all kinds of fags,Javion spoke to Malik and Alonzo,Malik and Alonzo still fooling around.Who,you talking

about that nigga with the dreads?
Alonzo questioned Javion.Yea,and
talk low man,dude can probably hear
you,Javion spoke to Alonzo.

Man fuck that nigga,let that nigga
think whatever he wanna think,but if
that nigga say some slick mad rude
shit out his mouth im going pop that
nigga with the quickness,and i want
that nigga to hear me,Alonzo spoke
to Javion,his face sort of
frowned.Dawg you probably like that
dread head nigga,talking about talk
low,you like that punk ass nigga
cuz,aint nobody stupid,you and

dreadlocks be kissy kissy,Malik spoke to Javion in a teasing manner.

Alonzo placed a short white towel around his naked waist as he slid his feet into a pair of thick flip flops and then headed slowly to Javion.Alonzo slowly and intimately and discreetly pushed himself and Javion into a corner of the huge house as their lips nearly met.Dude chill,what if dude see us and tell my mom dude,Javion spoke very silently to Alonzo as Alonzo moved himself up even closer to him as if he were ignoring his words,Javion fearing Quinton might catch them up close and personal in the quiet corner.

Quinton instantly turned his head away from Javion and Alonzo as he exited Pam's bedroom with his toolbox,his eyes catching a quick glimpse of Javion and Alonzo tightly pressed into the corner in an intimate position,a position many would assume was for a man and a woman.Dude he just saw us man,stop playing man,Javion whispered to Alonzo as Alonzo pressed up against him harder.Fuck that nigga cuz,you faking on me today dude,im just fucking around with you son,stop acting like a bitch dawg,Alonzo pressed himself up even harder to Javion,their foreheads and chests and above knee length towels and long exposed legs pressing tightly against each other,their lips seeming as if they wanted to make contact as well.

Javion tried to ease himself away from Alonzo but Alonzo pressed him harder to the wall,a serious and stern stare on his face.Stop playing with me dawg,Alonzo pressed Javion to the wall again as Javion began to fidget.Javion kissed Alonzo softly and quickly on the lips,hoping that if he did so in front of Quinton Alonzo would be offended by the exposure,but Alonzo was unfazed by it.Eww,he like kissing niggas cuz! Alonzo turned his head toward Quinton,hoping to embarrass Javion.Eww,look how he letting me kiss on him,nigga you gay,Alonzo began to forcefully kiss Javion in front of Quinton's tense watching eyes as he pressed Javion to the wall further.Javion finally shoved Alonzo from him as he readjusted the towel around his waist,his body tense.

Alonzo then quickly snatched Javion's towel off the waist of his naked body just as Javion was about to speak to Quinton,Javion quickly placing his towel back around his waist in annoyance as Alonzo and Malik snickered out loudly in response,Quinton in a state of quiet shock.Tell ms Pam i fixed her drain,im out now dawg,Quinton uttered slightly and tensely to Javion,his eyes only partly on Javion.Thanks man,Javion spoke to Quinton.No prob man,Quinton nodded back at Javion,and then headed out of the front door,placing the bottom lock on as he exited.Yall niggas wrong as fuck man,Javion spoke to Alonzo and Malik after Quinton left the house,his face slightly annoyed.

Javion then jumped slightly in shock as he heard three knocks tap against the door behind him.Oh shit,that shit scared me man! Javion spoke as he turned to the front door.Javion peeped out the peephole and saw that it was Quinton once again,and then opened the door.You alright,you left something? Javion spoke to Quinton with confusion.Yea,it was this metal piece in my toolbox,i dont see it in there no more,i think i left it in your moms bathroom,Quinton explained to Javion.Oh alright,come on in,Javion welcomed Quinton back into the house to find his missing tool.

Quinton headed down the hall to Pam's bedroom and then gave Javion a silent stare as he reached the end of the hall.Ay homey can you help me find the joint? Quinton spoke to Javion.Alright,here i come,Javion spoke as he headed down the hall to help Quinton find his missing tool piece.Quinton and Javion entered into the bathroom as Quinton suddenly shut the door behind them lightly,Javion's face becoming confused.Quinton silently nodded for Javion to come over as he bit down on his bottom lip.You get down like that cuz,like how them dudes out there was saying? Quinton questioned Javion very quietly as he and Javion stared eye to eye.

Chapter 6

Naw,them dudes be just fooling around and shit,Javion denied his same sex attraction to Quinton,his face slightly guilty and nervous.Oh,my bad then dude,i just wanted to know whats up,you feel where im coming from right? Quinton spoke smoothly to Javion as he clutched the crotch area of his jeans for Javion to see.Javion's eyes saw the huge print of Quinton's male genitals on the outside of the jeans as he pretended not to notice,Javion also noticing that there was never any missing tool,it was just Quinton's ploy to get him alone.

Quinton then began to rub his huge hands up and down Javion's exposed arms as he watched his facial expression.Quinton then slowly and smoothly took off his overshirt,revealing muscled arms and a set of abs that still showed through his grey tank top,Javion's eyes secretly liking what they saw.

I aint no lame ass nigga like them two niggas out there dawg,let me love on you cuz,my game is on point,Quinton spoke silently and seductively to

Javion as he licked his lips once,his
hands gently and tenderly caressing
Javion's arms and smooth abs.Ay cuz
if you not feeling this right now im
going just give you my number and
then maybe we can talk to each other
sometime,if you cool with that?
Quinton spoke to Javion.Alright,im
cool with that,Javion spoke softly and
silently and calmly to Quinton,Javion
playing it cool,tho he was blushing on
the inside.Javion saw a much more
subtle and gentlemen and mature
side of Quinton that he didn't see
much in Alonzo or Malik,tho they

both could be mature at times,but
not often.

I didn't mean to push up on you
dawg,i just wanted to let you know
im feeling you,here go my number,im
going put it in the medicine cabinet
so them niggas out there wont see
you come out with a piece of paper in
your hand and then get the
wondering and shit,Quinton spoke to
Javion as he wrote down his phone
number on a piece of torn paper
from his pocket and then placed it
inside the medicine cabinet above
the bathroom sink.I talk to you a little

later homeboy,Quinton spoke to Javion as he headed to the bathroom door to exit,Javion following behind him.

Javion and Quinton's eyes slightly widened in surprise as they accidently swatted Malik and Alonzo away with the bathroom door as it swung open to their listening ears,Alonzo and Malik flinching backwards as the bathroom door opened but then quickly catching their balance.Yall was listening to the door man? Javion questioned Malik and Alonzo.What if we was cuz,what you got something to hide bruh? Alonzo spoke to Javion.I aint got nothing to hide man,im a grown ass man dude,my business is my business,Javion spoke to Alonzo with slight annoyance.Who you talking to son,huh? Alonzo spoke to Javion as if he were scolding a child.Ay cuz,im about to leave yo,i dont want no trouble,stay cool man alright,and remember,Quinton spoke to Javion as he bumped his fist to his in a friendly gesture and then began to head for the front door.

Nigga i heard you and my mans in there talking that gay shit man,Alonzo blocked Quinton from heading to the door just as he was about to walk pass him,a frown on Alonzo's face,and his strong hand readjusting the towel around his waist.Dawg i dont want no trouble cuz,im not that nigga,Quinton spoke to Alonzo.Nigga i heard you and Javion whole conversation bruh man,i heard you trying get at dude,you disrespectful cuz,you coming up into his moms house and then trying hit on dude,you trying smash dude and shit cuz,you trifling for real nigga,dont come pass this joint again dawg,Alonzo spoke angrily to Quinton as he and Quinton both stared eye to eye in a stare down.

Dude get the fuck outta my way man! Quinton spoke angrily back to Alonzo.Cuz im telling you,you better not come back around here man,you dont just walk up in people house and think you own it cuz,and you dont try and smash the people that live there,thats just wrong dude,Alonzo spoke to Quinton,his fingers fidgeting tensely and then beginning to ball into fists.Dude what the fuck was that shit you was doing with homeboy earlier,you was kissing on dude like he was your bitch,whats up with that,since you wanna be nosy nigga,huh playboy,nigga yous a undercover faggot,what you mad because you think i scooped up dude from you? Quinton spoke to Alonzo with a smug smirk,Quinton knowing his words were getting to Alonzo.

Nigga buck up dawg,do something,punk ass nigga! Alonzo swung his right fist at Quinton,punching Quinton in the jaw as Quinton stood in shock and disbelief.Nigga you lost your fucking mind man! Quinton swung back at Alonzo,Alonzo ducking and dodging his blow quickly and swiftly and then placing up his dukes in a fighting stance as Quinton took off his overshirt,him and Quinton then exchanging swift and fast body blows.

Yall chill out man,Alonzo chill man,its not that serious! Javion quickly intervened in Alonzo and Quinton's fight.Let them duke that shit out cuz! Malik spoke to Javion,Malik wanting to let them fight.Naw man,now is not the time or place,Javion spoke to Malik.

Javion stepped inbetween Alonzo and Quinton and then guided Quinton to the front door.He aint worth it man,i get at you tho dude,i got you,stay safe,Javion soothed Quinton's anger as he escorted him out the front door,Javion knowing that if Quinton stayed he and Alonzo's fight would have intensified,Javion wanting to avoid anyone from getting severely hurt in their brawl.

Chapter 7

Dude you always starting shit,Javion spoke to Alonzo after Quinton left the house.Nigga who is you talking to man? Alonzo spoke angrily to Javion as he approached him.Nigga im talking to you,nigga i aint scared of you! Javion spoke to Alonzo boldly as they got closer and closer to each other in anger.Dawg you must be talking to somebody else,because you cant be talking to me dude?! Alonzo spoke to Javion.

Nigga you is a hoe ass nigga man,you just let any motherfuckers run up in you,you worser than some females i know dawg,yea,i heard yall in the bathroom dawg,i heard every motherfucking thing,you know what,let me go handle some shit right quick! Alonzo spoke to Javion angrily,and then quickly heading into the bathroom,Javion quickly following behind him,Javion knowing what he was after.Give me my shit dawg! Javion commanded Alonzo as Alonzo snatched Quinton's phone number from out of the bathroom cabinet.Im going flush this shit,play with me! Alonzo dangled the tiny piece of paper with Quinton's phone number on it over the toilet,and then dropping it in as he flushed it,Quinton's phone number now nowhere in sight.

Nigga what the fuck is wrong with you?! Javion yelled at Alonzo.Nigga who the fuck is you talking to dawg?! Alonzo shoved Javion into the living area against the wall,fury in his eyes.Dude you better get outta my face man,im serious,Javion warned Alonzo,Alonzo ignoring him.Get your hands off me nigga! Javion angrily shoved Alonzo back,a more aggressive side coming out of Javion.

Both Javion and Alonzo stood tall with their chests poked out to each other and their foreheads touching,their wide and broad shoulders knocking and the fabric of their short above knee length white towels grazing,and their exposed thighs pressing,and their showers shoes and thick flip flops almost clashing.What you wanna hit me dude? Javion spoke to Alonzo as they continued to stare each other down closely eye to eye,frustration on their handsome faces.

Stop playing with me cuz,stop fucking playing with me man! Alonzo swiftly shoved Javion to the wall with the force of his tall body,his fists balled.What nigga,what you thought i was weak?! Javion spoke to Alonzo as he shoved Alonzo back with just as much force.Little faggot ass nigga,dawg im trying my best not to beat the bullshit out you right now cuz,you got me all fucked up cuz! Alonzo yelled angrily at Javion as they stood face to face.Dude why is you so

fucking heated right now man?!
Javion shouted at Alonzo.Nigga you
acting up right now cuz,you fucking
up,this aint Javion im talking to right
now cuz,it cant be! Alonzo spoke
angrily to Javion.

Lonzo chill man,i know how you be
dawg,nigga you just want some ass
and head nigga,and you thought
dreads dude was getting it,you
thought dreads nigga was about to
crack that shit,Malik spoke to Alonzo
with a slight smirk.Nigga this aint no
joking matter man,im about to go to J
body man,real talk cuz! Alonzo spoke

angrily to Malik,using Javion's nickname,Malik then just watching from the sideline as Alonzo and Javion continued to argue.Man you letting that dread head nigga fuck with your head cuz,because i know you aint talking to me man,that nigga aint shit dawg,nigga aint got my swag cuz,your faggot ass just probably wanna suck his dick man,that shit is nasty cuz,that nigga aint better than nobody cuz! Alonzo yelled at Javion with intense anger and emotion.

Man im not going do this with you tonight man,im going to bed,im out,i see yall in the morning,Javion turned his back to Alonzo to head off to his bedroom.Nigga dont you ever walk away from me like that cuz,ay man what the fuck is wrong with you son,what the fuck is wrong with you cuz,huh?! Alonzo swiftly and forcefully snatched Javion back around by his exposed shoulder,his thumb pressing tightly onto the flesh of Javion's neck.

Alonzo had become slightly possessive of Javion,his lustful and sexual experimentations with Javion growing beyond what he had imagined.Javion,Alonzo,and Malik didn't think about the certain strings that came along with lust and passion,they never once thought that sometimes feelings could become involved.

Chill Lonzo,you a little taller than him man,thats our new homey man! Malik quickly rushed over to Alonzo to stop him from gripping Javion,Malik seeing that Javion and Alonzo's arguement was getting slightly violent and out of control.Naw,let me go Malik,get the fuck off me dude,im going just talk to homey,he faking on me right now dude! Alonzo spoke to Malik as Malik restrained him.Nigga you only good for a nut dawg,you aint shit cuz,faggot ass nigga,i aint tripping off you nigga! Alonzo shouted at Javion,Alonzo lying to Javion and himself as he tried to break free of Malik's grip to get to Javion.Fuck you man,fuck you Alonzo! Javion spoke to Alonzo.Naw nigga,i fucked you cuz,i was all up in you nigga,and your gay ass liked it cuz,talking about some fuck me! Alonzo yelled to Javion.

Alonzo was used to dealing with submissive females in his love affairs,but Javion wasn't so easily submissive,and he wasn't female,but male,Javion being more of a challenge to Alonzo made Alonzo angry but it also made him want Javion even more,the thrill of cat and mouse games.Dawg you hurting man,i can hear that shit in your voice cuz,Malik spoke to Alonzo as he continued to restrain him.Man that nigga aint shit to me dawg,he think i give a fuck about him,man i dont give a fuck about him,he a dude,i like females,females cuz,fuck i look like getting hyped over a nigga for dude! Alonzo shouted to Malik,his eyes now glassy.

Let that shit out cuz,you hurting man,you caught feelings for dude dawg,keep that shit a hundred man,its alright cuz,but just calm down my nigga,Malik spoke warmly to Alonzo as Alonzo began to settle down.Man i got mad love for that nigga man,and he going fake on me for that dread head nigga tho,thats bullshit man! Alonzo explained to Malik as his voice began to crack,deep emotion on his face,Alonzo feeling the full affects of what it was to be a scorned lover,Alonzo getting a taste of the passion he and Javion shared and now wanting to keep it to himself.

Javion stared at Alonzo with slight remorse and guilt,Javion feeling as if he took advantage of Alonzo's young and inexperienced emotions,and shattering them in the process.

Chapter 8

Man i didn't mean to hurt you dude,i thought we was all just having a good time man,you stated yourself just now that you like girls,so i dont think im in the wrong to keep myself guarded dude,i just look at you as a homeboy,you know,a homeboy who i fuck with every now and then,Javion explained calmly to Alonzo,Alonzo listening.

Dawg none of us niggas knew what the fuck was going go down the moment we smashed son,stop acting dumb dawg,but its about respect my nigga,you cant say oh i roll with these niggas and im going roll with this nigga next,you gotta choose my dude,thats all im saying cuz,im cool with you smashing Malik,but im not too cool on you smashing other niggas cuz,keep this shit between us,no outside niggas,dawg im a thorough nigga,that shit in my blood cuz,homeboy came up in here trying get at one of my homeboys like he was about that life,i dont play that shit son,i dont cuz,you should know me by now,Alonzo spoke to Javion.I understand how you feeling man,but if i did the same thing to you you would have probably checked me dude,dont lie,Javion spoke to Alonzo.

Dawg in all honesty i would have respected where you was coming from cuz,dont try and change shit around man,i hate niggas that do that,we talking about what went down tonight dude,Alonzo spoke to Javion.Javion i aint going lie tho dawg,but i did feel kind of disrespected by that dread head nigga flow cuz,you like fam cuz,you dont try and get at niggas fam right in front of them or behind their back and shit,like how he was doing,he was doing that shit on a slick tip,that made me feel some kind of way cuz,he was mad disrespectful for that,thats my piece on this shit,and now im going get quiet my niggas,Malik spoke to Javion.Dawg when i used to fuck my bitches i refused for another nigga to run up in them right after i got done smashing it cuz,its a certain code you take man,shit disrespectful,Alonzo spoke to Javion.

I got yall,i got yall,trust me i do,but i have a say so too,Javion spoke to both Alonzo and Malik.And we cool with that cuz,but just try and do right by your homeboys,we are your homeboys,you dont go against your homeys son,you should've been down with me,and not that other nigga dude,Alonzo spoke to Javion.Dawg you acted like you wanted to beat my ass tho dude,like seriously tho,i thought me and you was going duke it out man,Javion spoke to Alonzo.My bad cuz,my intentions wasn't to lay hands on you but when you walked away from a nigga like i wasn't nothing to you that shit got me heated man,i did wanna pop you a few times homey,but like i said,my bad,i got much love for you man,Alonzo spoke to Javion in a warm and calm voice.

Can i get a hug? Javion spoke softly to Alonzo.I got you cuz,aint a thing,Alonzo spoke to Javion as he gave him a huge bearhug,Alonzo's breath beating down Javion's neck.Alonzo then planted a soft kiss on Javion's cheek as they continued to hug tightly.And i still got dude phone number memorized nigga,Javion playfully teased Alonzo as they hugged,Alonzo snickering silently in response.

Javion and Alonzo then bumped their fists together in a friendly gesture after their hug was over,Malik joining in as well.Javion placed Quinton's memorized phone number into his cellphone as he silently memorized it by heart,his eyes and thoughts remembering the exact numbers Quinton had written down on the now flushed piece of paper.Man im horny as fuck cuz,i aint bust a nut in a hot minute man,Alonzo spoke to Javion with a subliminal message behind his words,his hand slightly squeezing onto the crotch area of his towel as his eyes stared at Javion intimately.

Man let's go chill in my room,we can play the game or something,Javion welcomed Alonzo and Malik into his bedroom.Nigga fuck the game,im trying get a phat ass nut dawg,Alonzo spoke to Javion.Shit,i aint got a nut in a minute either,Malik spoke to Javion.We can do some things in my room,and that way my mom wont catch us if she was to pop up like last time,Javion smirked at Alonzo and Malik.Javion then headed into his bedroom as Alonzo and Malik followed behind him,Malik closing and locking Javion's bedroom door after they all entered,their naked bodies still only covered with nothing but short white towels around their waists and shower shoes and thick flip flops on their feet.

Javion laid himself down onto his bed as Alonzo towered over him.Alonzo eased his exposed crotch near Javion's face as he removed the towel from his naked waist.Open your mouth cuz,Alonzo ordered Javion as he chucked his huge penis into his hand,his naked body still hovering above Javion's staring eyes.Alonzo dipped himself down into Javion's mouth as Javion took him in in gagging gulps.Im going fuck that face dawg,Alonzo moaned out silently to Javion as he continued to dip his hard penis back and forth and in and out of Javion's mouth,Javion's tongue gliding up the shaft of it each time it drilled down into his warm mouth.

Alonzo then rested himself deeply inside of Javion's full mouth,Alonzo keeping himself casually well placed into Javion's mouth as he laid there on top of Javion's face,his penis not allowing Javion the chance to come up for air,Javion's hands caressing Alonzo's tight and hard buttocks as he sat there with a mouthful of Alonzo,the room silent and only filled with gurgling sounds.

Alonzo began to thrust himself as if he was making love to Javion's face,Alonzo's hand then reaching down to pull off Javion's towel.Alonzo then slowly slipped his wet penis from Javion's mouth as he positioned himself inside of Javion as Javion moaned out in a gasp.Alonzo gripped Javion's neck tightly as he began to thrust himself relentlessly back and forth into Javion's naked body,Javion's voice vibrating to the strong and rocky motions of he and Alonzo's nude bodies fleshly connecting harshly and pleasurably.

Im recording,Malik smirked with his tongue out the side of his mouth as he began to film Javion and Alonzo having sexual intercourse with Javion's camera phone.Stop playing dawg,take that shit off my face cuz! Alonzo spoke to Malik with annoyance as Malik continued.Dude you play too much,cut that shit off!

Javion then spoke to Malik,Malik neither obeying Javion nor Alonzo as he kept filming them in excitement.We should send this shit to homeboy,dude with dreads! Malik spoke to Alonzo and Javion with a wide and sneaky smile,Alonzo then pushing back and forth into Javion harder as if he was giving the camera a show.This how you dick a nigga down dawg,Alonzo began to thrust himself into Javion in all kinds of positions as Javion moaned out deeply,Malik still filming.

Malik only filmed the bottom half of Javion and Alonzo's naked bodies,but made sure to leave their faces out of the video recording.Put the camera on dude face,only his mouth nigga,let that nigga see my work,Alonzo commanded Malik as Malik placed the recording camera phone above Javion's moaning lips,Alonzo then pumping Javion harder as the camera phone focused on Javion's gasping and moaning stuttering lips departing.

Put the camera on my dick dawg,im about to bust! Alonzo quickly ordered

Malik as Malik then placed the recording camera phone on Javion and Alonzo's exposed bottom halves again,the camera phone recording Alonzo's thick hard penis slamming back and forth into Javion and then exploding semen all over Javion's naked abs and body as both Alonzo and Javion moaned out in pleasure.Shit,fuck that,im about to get my nut too,Malik then began to stroke himself above Javion as he dropped his towel to the bedroom floor,Malik adding himself into the video.Malik shoot thick semen onto Javion's already semen soaked and wet nude abs as he moaned out in deep thrills of pleasure.

Your boy just got creamed by two dicks dude,hope you like the video my nigga,he liked it too,that ass was tight too! Alonzo spoke to the camera phone as it recorded both his and Malik's huge exposed slinky hard penises beating and spanking against Javion's wet and naked body and abs as if they were disciplining him.We out dawg,and that nut was good as fuck homey,Malik then spoke into the camera phone without showing his face,and then turning it off,the on light of the camera phone then dimming down to no light at all as it cut off.

Send that shit to homeboy dawg,Alonzo spoke to Malik,Alonzo wanting Malik to send the sexually explicit recorded video of himself,Javion,and Malik to Quinton,Alonzo hoping to upset Quinton,Alonzo knowing that Quinton had a romantic interest in Javion.Man you better not send that shit dude,Javion spoke to Malik in an exhausted voice.Dawg just let me send it cuz,please son,Malik begged

Javion,Malik eager to send their video to Quinton.

Javion quickly got up from under Alonzo as he snatched his camera phone cellphone from Malik's fingers,Javion sending the video by accident as his finger accidently touched the send button on his camera phone,Javion gasping in regret,fear,shock,and horror.Oh shit dawg,you then sent that joint cuz! Malik snickered out to Javion as Alonzo snickered out as well,Javion's face in shock of his quick and fast accident.Dawg chill,it's not like our faces on that shit dawg,Alonzo spoke to Javion with a grin.

Javion received a text message from Quinton two hours later after his accidental sending of he and Alonzo and Malik's explicit recorded video.Javion read Quinton's text message silently to himself as Malik read it out loud,the text message reading dude i thought you was cool people,but i guess you one of them dick hungry niggas,one of them thirsty ass bottom niggas,that could've been my dick in you,you foul dawg,the text read.

javion was highly offended and shaken by Quinton's text message,but for some odd reason he found humor in it as well,Javion feeling he did something spontaneous,fun,and wild.That nigga heated cuz! Alonzo spoke to Javion and Malik with a smirk,Javion and Malik then smirking as well.Javion,Alonzo,and Malik all smirked silently for a few seconds together and then finally bursted into loud laughter and humor.

Javion's bedroom was filled with he and Alonzo and Malik's snickers for more than minutes,but they continued a strong and wild and sexually adventurous brotherhood for years,and years to come.

The end.

www.ingramcontent.com/pod-product-compliance
Lightning Source LLC
Chambersburg PA
CBHW051432280526
45785CB00003B/1254

* 9 7 8 1 3 1 2 2 9 8 8 3 5 *